Refocus

G000017855

JESUS
THE JEW

David Spriggs
with James Crossley

Bible Society
Stonehill Green
Westlea
Swindon SN5 7DG
biblesociety.org.uk
bibleresources.org.uk

First published 2013 by The British and Foreign Bible Society.

ISBN: 978-0-564-04876-2

Production by Bible Society Resources Ltd, a wholly-owned subsidiary
of The British and Foreign Bible Society
Cover and text design by Colin Hall, TypeFunction

Printed in Great Britain

Contents

Contents

INTRODUCTION

We are truly excited to be able to make this study guide available to you. It is a collaboration between biblical scholars, especially Prof. James Crossley of University of Sheffield Biblical Studies Department and Bible Society. By working in partnership we can help scholarly research stimulate ordinary Christians, to enrich our minds and hearts. These sessions are prepared with church home groups and similar contexts particularly in mind.

What are these studies for?

Through these studies we will be refreshing our understanding of who Jesus was in his own context – focusing on the Jewishness of Jesus.

We will note, for instance, that when Jesus was engaging in very vigorous debates with the Pharisees about 'the Law', he was not necessarily being rude or aggressive, but was debating within the normal 'conventions' – rather like Prime Minister's Question Time in the House of Commons. In turn this might prompt us to think about the validity of frank debate about important matters of faith and Christian behaviour.

We will also explore how Jesus was perceived and how he saw himself, both vital issues for us as Christians.

Why these studies really matter

As we see more clearly the Jewishness of Jesus and understand his words and actions more fully, we can enrich our relationship with Jesus today.

- It will help to ensure that the picture of Jesus we all inevitably develop, and through which we relate spiritually to him, is as accurate as possible.

- It will lead to a better understanding of both the context and the meaning of the biblical text at some critical places.

- We will be less likely to project unhelpful stereotypes from the Gospels into our contemporary consciousness – which, for example, has sometimes led to anti-Semitism.

Content of the studies

In six sessions we will explore together six different aspects of the Jewishness of Jesus.

1. Jesus in his world – and some of the groups which surrounded him.

2. Jesus and the Law – wealth.

3. Jesus and the Law – divorce.

4. Jesus through others' eyes – 'Who do people say that I am?' – some categories that people used as they tried to understand who Jesus was.

5. Jesus through his own eyes – 'Who do you say that I am?' – looking at a range of understandings of the term 'Messiah' which would have coloured the views of both the disciples and Jesus himself.

6. Jesus and prayer, especially the Lord's Prayer.

We will link these in with our own experience of contemporary life.

How the sessions work

While particularly important for group leaders, we suggest that everyone involved in this biblical journey of exploration reads the following introductory notes.

For group leaders

Leading

Your focus should always be to lead your group in the most helpful and appropriate way.

- If it is a new group, you will probably want to encourage people to introduce themselves before the first session gets fully underway.

- For any group, you may want to have some spare Bibles ready in case people forget their own.

- Encourage everyone to become involved in the conversation, and gently control those who may tend to dominate it.

- It is often helpful to include prayer early on in a session, but it is up to you whether you choose to do that right at the start, or after the 'opening experience', or elsewhere.

- Please feel free to adapt and use the material in ways that best help your group.

Continuity

Some groups have one leader throughout, but others prefer to rotate the leading. In the latter case, please take extra care about continuity.

- Some people may have missed the previous session, so it can be helpful to start with a brief recap.

- Some people may have carried out an activity or research between sessions. Providing opportunities for them to feed back may be good for the whole group – but be careful about time.

- At the end of the session, alert people to the next topic and encourage them to familiarise themselves with the content.

Suggested timings

Assuming you have an hour for your session, suggested timings for each part of the process are indicated in brackets below. Please adjust proportionally if you are planning a shorter or longer session.

Opening experience (15 minutes)

This allows us to engage with some aspect of the topic which will be explored later through the key Bible passage(s). It is an integral part of the whole learning experience – as well as acting as an ice-breaker, initiating conversations and helping to develop relationships and deeper understanding between group members.

Each 'opening experience' has been carefully crafted to affirm the importance of people's own experiences and reflections on the life issues to which the biblical material relates. This will help to increase a sense of the significance of the topic which is to be explored by the whole group.

The 'opening experience' will also enable those with less biblical literacy to make a vital contribution to the group's learning. If handled well, such a group activity will create a real alertness and eagerness for the biblical encounter to come.

Bible encounter (30 minutes)

In our 'Bible encounter' we will look at one or more passages from the Gospels. Sometimes additional notes or resources for further study will also be included. It is important that the Bible passages take centre stage. Often there is one particular passage to focus on – the 'key passage' – and there are many ways to help the group take in its significance.

- One person can read the whole passage.

- The passage can be broken up into sections and different voices (even different translations) used for the reading.

- Sometimes it is helpful to leave a pause of 30 seconds between the sections, so that people can recall or 'live in' that section before moving on.

- Group members can be asked to follow the passage in their own Bibles and, if the translation is different, to comment on the differences they notice.

- People can be asked to close their eyes and simply listen to the passage. Bible Society's recording **YGTT (You've Got the Time)**, read by professionals, can add another dimension.

- The group can read the passage silently before discussions begin.

YGTT is available to download free from biblesociety.org.uk/ygtt

Using a variety of approaches over the six sessions can help add interest and keep things fresh. The important thing is to ensure that group members pay careful attention to the key passage, so that it is the focus of the discussions that follow.

Group discussion questions (15 minutes)

This section provides questions for the group to help them engage together with the 'Bible encounter'. There is no need to deal with all the questions, nor all at the same depth.

- As leader you may have sensed through the 'Bible encounter' section which questions are most significant for your group.

- Alternatively, you could ask the group which questions they want to work with.

- Sometimes you could split the group and ask each smaller group to work on different questions.

Suggestions for reflection

These are intended to help anyone wishing to continue to engage with the issues raised on their own outside the group. For those groups who want to meet more frequently, they could form the basis of a more open or less structured conversation. There is usually one idea for some kind of action and another for prayer.

At the end of some sessions, additional study resources are also suggested.

Preparation

- We hope that you will familiarise yourself with the content of each session well beforehand, so that you have time to check details if you need to do so.

- Text panels offering more detailed information on aspects of each topic are spread throughout the session pages. You may find it useful to engage with this extra material before the group meets. Often it may not be necessary to share or discuss these details with the group, but it offers an extra resource to draw on if necessary.

- Asking God to help and guide you, as well as praying for the members of your group, is also an excellent practice.

Protocol

From time to time relevant websites are offered as a resource. This raises a question of group 'etiquette'. It might be stimulating and helpful if someone with a smartphone or laptop can access these websites while the group is operating. However, in some groups this might be seen as impolite or as a distraction, so it would be advisable to clarify this protocol with your group right at the start.

Pastoral support

Occasionally the issue covered might cause pastoral needs to surface. Sessions 2 and 3 on wealth and divorce respectively are obvious possibilities in this regard. There is no need to be over-anxious about the challenges that may arise. Jesus frequently seems to have brought disturbance, so we can hardly expect it to be otherwise today! Nevertheless, understanding, kindness and support are vital components of a good experience in a group. So please support people for whom these are sensitive matters, and if necessary help them to link with others in the church who can provide more specialised help.

For members

Every member of the group has an important contribution to make.

- Be willing to share your own experiences on a number of issues, to the extent that you feel comfortable doing so.

- Carefully read (or listen to) the biblical passages and other material. Each of us is likely to discern different things from the passages and the topic as a whole, and sharing these discoveries will benefit everyone.

- Within the group, always try to 'respond well'. This includes being prompt in attending meetings, being sensitive to other members and encouraging them by listening attentively and sympathetically. Such responses can greatly enhance everyone's experience and learning.

- Allow the group leader(s) to guide and shape the study time. It is also good to pray for your leader(s) as they prepare for each session and lead the group.

- Bringing a Bible, and occasionally other things as requested, indicates real involvement. Through this demonstration of commitment, other members will gain an enhanced sense of the value of the time spent together.

INTRODUCTORY SESSION

This material can be used for an introductory session for the group, or simply read personally as background material.

First impressions can shape us throughout our lifetime. Many children's Bibles and pictures depicting Jesus (especially from the Victorian period or the first half of the 20th century) present him as having typically Western features and either nut-brown or blond long hair. Given this background, and some of the well-known hymns about Jesus, it is easy for us to see him through traditional 'Western Christian' lenses and so run the danger of distorting the understanding we have of Jesus.

If, however, we take the incarnation seriously, this involves appreciating that first and foremost Jesus was a Jew living at the beginning of what has become known as the 'Christian Era'. The six Bible studies that follow will help to reconnect us with this vital aspect of the reality of Jesus. In addition they will enable us to discern sometimes new, sometimes fascinating and sometimes challenging insights about Jesus.

In the last few decades, through archaeology, anthropology and sociology, as well as through more standard historical approaches, a richer understanding of Judaism in the time of Jesus has been emerging. This helps us to see Jesus more vividly within his own culture. In turn this provides us with a richer and probably more accurate understanding of what he said and did and who he was. This is the exciting and important journey we are now taking together.

In order to prepare us for our journey of discovery, it might be helpful to start by thinking about different visual images of Jesus. The following activity suggests ways of doing this.

 **Opening experience**

Either

Do a Google search for images of Jesus, or visit websites such as http://spiritlessons.com/Documents/Jesus_Pictures/ Jesus_Christ_Pictures.htm. Compare these with images shown at http://www.rejesus.co.uk/site/module/faces_of_jesus/.

Or

Ask someone to print out different images of Jesus and bring them to the group.

Or

Invite people to bring to the group one or more images or pictures of Jesus they like.

Then

Take time to look at the various pictures of Jesus.

- Explore together which images you like and why.

- Reflect on similarities and differences. Why are the images as they are? What are they reflecting most – the Bible, the context from which they come, or both? What are they trying to communicate about Jesus?

- Do these differences matter? Does this variety make the Bible less or more important?

- Close with a reading from the Gospels (such as Luke 8.40-42, 8.49-56, 9.51-56, 19.1-10) and pray for each other – that as we discover more about Jesus we may become more like him.

Glimpsing Jesus' World

Introduction

In this session we explore some of the groups of people Jesus had to deal with – those he lived amongst. One very famous passage about Jesus is John 1.1–14. There we read, 'He came to what was his own ... And the Word became flesh and lived among us' (verses 11,14 NRSV).

The Gospels indicate that Jesus grew up in Nazareth but also knew Jerusalem. Nazareth was a small town or large village close to the relatively cosmopolitan town of Sepphoris within the province of Galilee. Galileans were sometimes regarded with suspicion by Jerusalem Jews. Jerusalem was the political and religious capital. Jesus was taken there to be presented in the temple and circumcised, and he is depicted later as engaging with the teachers in the temple. Thus physically and culturally Jesus was embedded in the heart of Jewish society and faith. There were many different groups he would frequently meet.

 ## Opening experience

Objective: to develop group members' awareness that any 'society' is more complex than is normally perceived.

- How might you describe the various groups within your church? You might label them 'Prayer Book' or 'Fresh Expressions'; 'Evangelical' or 'Catholic'; 'Charismatic' or

'Conservative'; 'Hymn Book' or 'Song Singers'; 'old' or 'young'; 'women in leadership' or 'men only in leadership', and so on. Why do we use such labels? When are they helpful and when not? When are they misleading?

- How can you cross over from 'your group' to others? And how can you help others to do the same?

- Do you have friends in 'other groups'? If not, why not? If so, what does this do to your evaluation of the 'other group'?

- What does your discussion suggest about the likely accuracy of our understanding of the complexities of society in first-century Palestine?

 Bible encounter

There are many different groups mentioned in the Gospels. These form our understanding of the sets of people Jesus encountered. The main ones are listed below.

- Pharisees, scribes and teachers of the Law

- Sadducees

- Priests (chief priests, elders, Levites)

- Herodians

- Tax collectors

- Sinners

- The poor

- The crowd

Together as a group try to recall other named 'collections' of people who are mentioned in the Gospels.

Some of the group names refer to the powerful figures in society, often religious leaders; others are used derogatively; still others cover sometimes the same and sometimes overlapping groups.

Using our key passage, we will look at some of the powerful groups who feature in the Gospel accounts of Jesus' life, namely the Pharisees, Sadducees and Herodians. Through their interaction these groups help to define the distinctiveness of Jesus, because they are often presented as being in confrontation with him.

Pharisees, scribes and teachers of the Law: Mark 7.1–5; Matthew 23.23; Luke 13.31–33; Mark 12.28–34 (notice that 'teacher' can also be applied to Jesus, Matthew 8.19)
Sadducees: Mark 12.18–27
Herodians: Mark 3.6; 12.13
Priests (chief priests, elders, Levites): Luke 1.5–17; Luke 10.29–37; Mark 11.15–18
Tax collectors: Mark 2.13–17; Luke 18.9–13; Luke 19.1–9
Sinners: Mark 2.15–18; Matthew 11.19; Mark 14.41
The poor: Matthew 5.3, 11.5; Luke 4.18; Mark 12.41–44; Luke 14.12–14
The crowd: Mark 2.14; 10.1; 15.11

Other groups who would become known as Zealots and Sicarii are, at most, only hinted at within the Gospels (see Luke 6.15–16). These were the 'terrorists' of their time – committed to direct resistance against Rome or its rulers. Additionally there were 'the brigands', either patriotic or economic robbers (Mark 15.7). Then there are 'the Essenes', who are mentioned by Josephus (see below), and the Qumran Community, famous for the Dead Sea Scrolls, who are not mentioned in the Gospels or Josephus.

 ## Key passage: Mark 12.13–28

In this passage we meet the crowd, Pharisees, Sadducees, Herodians and a scribe. Let's take a closer look at the three main groups.

Pharisees

The Pharisees were said to have numbered at least 6,000 in the time of Jesus. They developed and applied the Mosaic laws (laws of Moses). Dispersed throughout Israel, they were probably losing some of their political influence to the Sadducees, which may have contributed to their anxiety about the potential threat which Jesus posed. They were also involved with synagogue worship. A few were members of the Sanhedrin (the Jewish legal council), and many were *scribes* and *teachers of the Law* (see below). They were religiously nationalistic. Later most were opposed to the rebellions against Rome. Eventually their approaches became synonymous with Judaism. The rabbis are seen as their successors.

What is not obvious from the Gospels is that there were significant divisions among the Pharisees, some (often the wealthier ones) taking a much stricter approach (the Hillel school) than others (the Shammai school).

The designation *scribes* emphasises the role of preserving the Scriptures and the developments of the Mosaic law, as well as the responsibility for administration in the Sanhedrin. Many scribes were either Pharisees or closely associated with them.

Teachers of the Law were much the same as scribes – the terms are more or less synonymous. Although priests were also involved in interpreting and applying the Law, they were not usually denoted by this term.

It is also worth noting that Matthew 8.19 suggests that not all Pharisees were opposed to Jesus. Another point of interest is that Luke 13.31–33 indicates that the Pharisees also had access to Herod.

Sadducees

The Sadducees' origins are disputed, but they seem to have come from the ruling wealthy aristocrats, probably with Jerusalem connections. The majority of the Sanhedrin were Sadducees, as were the high priests. They disappeared after the revolts against Rome and the destruction of Jerusalem around 70 AD.

The Sadducees held strictly to the value of the Torah. According to Josephus, they believed in free will, but they rejected any belief in the resurrection (possibly including the restoration of Israel).

Sometimes in the Gospels the Pharisees are associated with the Sadducees (Matthew 3.7; 16.1,11–12) and sometimes they are distinguished from each other (Matthew 22.34–35). Matthew describes the one who approaches Jesus as 'a lawyer' (22.35), whereas Mark describes him as 'a scribe' (12.28). Again, these are more or less synonyms.

Herodians

The Herodians are thought to be a group who favoured the Herodian dynasty and saw Herod Antipas as the legitimate ruler of the Jews. We have no knowledge of them outside the Gospels.

Their association with the Pharisees (see Mark 7.1–5, Matthew 23.23, Luke 13.31–33, Mark 12.28–34, Matthew 8.19) is normally taken as an arrangement of convenience (united by a common enemy), but others see this (especially the second) as indicating that they agreed with the Pharisees in taking a nationalistic stance in opposition to Roman rule.

Josephus

We have accounts of some of these groups in Josephus, a Jewish historian rather influenced by pro-Roman tendencies. He mentions the Pharisees and Sadducees along with 'the Essenes', whom we do not meet in the Gospels. He does not mention the Herodians.

> ...the Pharisees have delivered to the people a great many observances by succession from their fathers, which are not written in the laws of Moses; and for that reason it is that the Sadducees reject them, and say that we are to esteem those observances to be obligatory which are in the written word, but are not to observe what are derived from the tradition of our forefathers. And concerning these things it is that great disputes and differences have arisen among them, while the Sadducees are able to persuade none but the rich, and have not the populace favourable to them, but the Pharisees have the multitude on their side.
>
> (Josephus, *Antiquities of the Jews*, 13.297–298)

Our precise grasp of who was in any group and how they behaved is sometimes made more difficult by an apparent lack of clarity in the Gospels. For instance, Mark 12.1,12,13 uses 'them' and 'they'. Look at Mark 11.27 and 12.13 and compare these with the parallel passages in Matthew 21.23,45 and 22.15. Also different Gospels refer to different groups (or use different group descriptors) when clearly the same situation is envisaged, e.g. Matthew 16.6 (Pharisees and Sadducees); Luke 12.1 (Pharisees only); and a variant reading in Mark 8.15 (Pharisees and Herodians).

Group discussion questions

For each of the groups mentioned above – Pharisees (together with scribes and teachers of the Law), Saducees, and Herodians – consider together the following questions.

1. What insights do you gain about the group from the Bible passages?

2. How do you think they perceived Jesus?

3. How did Jesus view them?

4. How did Jesus differ from them (think of behaviour as well as beliefs)?

If you have time, look at Matthew 23 and read the 'woes' that are attributed to Jesus against the scribes and Pharisees.

1. How do you respond to these?

2. Why do you think Jesus did not address the Saducees or the Herodians in a similar way?

 Suggestions for reflection

- Read one or more Gospels to gain greater clarity about the groups referred to, whether by name or pronoun. If possible, make a list of them all.

- Pray for the various groups or factions in your church community in the light of Jesus' prayer that we may all be one.

Resources for further study

Consult any contemporary dictionary of the Bible to glean more details of groups that particularly interest you. See, for instance, Joel B Green, Scot McKnight and I Howard Marshall (eds), *Dictionary of Jesus and the Gospels* (IVP, 1992); Craig Evans (ed.), *The Routledge Encyclopedia of the Historical Jesus* (Routledge, 2010).

Jesus and the Law: Wealth

Introduction

One of the complex but critical requirements for understanding Jesus properly in his Jewish setting is to discover his attitude to the Jewish Law or Torah. We will be exploring this in the next two sessions.

When people are talking or writing about 'Jewish Law' in general, we can distinguish three things.

1. The Mosaic Law – the Torah, the first five books in our Bible

2. The Halakah – the laws that were developed on the basis of the Torah

3. The interpretation of these laws as presented in the Mishnah (compiled by about 200 AD) and later still the Talmud

Understanding the Torah and the development of the Law were matters of intense debate. That ongoing debate was not eradicated from the records we have, but was kept and accumulated to indicate the wealth of understandings which the Torah generated.

Within the early Christian communities there were other kinds of debate about the Law, including its overall function with respect to salvation, the formation of the Christian communities and their relationship to the Jews.

Christian writers and preachers have often presented Jesus (and certainly Paul) as being opposed to the Jewish Law. Yet more recent studies have emphasised that Jesus, at least, falls

---

It may be helpful to understand the following terms associated with Jewish Law and its interpretation.

The Torah: narrowly, this refers to the laws of the first five books of the Bible, but sometimes the term is extended to refer to the whole of the Old Testament. There was also a view that alongside the written Law there was an oral Torah as well, originally given to Moses.

Midrash: teaching which forms a running commentary on scriptural texts, including attention to single words, grammar and similarities to other passages. This was intended to extend the application of the original passages to keep them relevant but not to change the meaning.

The Haggadah: scriptural interpretation which is non-legal, aimed at increasing motivation for keeping the Law and the development of piety. It includes parables, fables, prayers and proverbs.

The Halakah: a collection of talmudic and rabbinic literature relating to religious and civil practices – essentially interpretation and reinterpretation of Jewish Law. As such it expressed authoritatively the aims and practices of Jewish life. Originally much of this was oral and became attributed to Moses.

The Mishnah: an important written collection of rabbinic laws, supplementary to the Torah, formed between 120 and 200 AD.

The Talmud: two versions exist, a shorter one (Jerusalem) and a longer one (Babylonian). Each contains the commentary of later rabbis on the Mishnah and runs into several volumes.

within a pattern of approaches to the Mosaic Law that would have seemed 'normal' to his contemporaries. Vehement debate was common within groups of Pharisees. James Crossley writes:

> There was a great deal of diversity and (sometimes violent) debate over ... the Torah ... Some recent work is showing that Jesus' views on the Law were all paralleled in early Judaism.
>
> (James Crossley, *The New Testament and Jewish Law*, T&T Clark, 2010, page 116)

> Such groups (e.g. the Pharisees) were liable to fall out and engage in heated debate, perhaps even violent debate, over the nature of legal interpretation.
>
> (ibid., page 25)

Within the Gospels we can see many significant issues which the Law covered, such as family, purity, non-violence and wealth. Often they present Jesus as operating in a relatively conventional Jewish way, with respect to individual laws and the Law as a whole. Wealth is a significant topic for us all.

 ## Opening experience

Objective: to stimulate awareness of the ambivalent attitudes many of us may have towards wealth.

- Name some really wealthy people who are national or international figures or celebrities. If possible, bring some pictures and stories from newspapers, or ask people to recall who has featured in the news recently.

- What advantages or disadvantages does wealth bring these people?

- Does the way people have (a) obtained and (b) used their wealth influence the way we view them? For instance, have they earned their wealth (Richard Branson, Bill Gates), inherited their wealth (Queen Elizabeth II), been lucky (discovering the Stafford Hoard, or winning the National Lottery), or obtained wealth by dubious or criminal means?

Consider our attitudes to wealth

②

• Do people in the group view wealth as a blessing or a
  curse? Does it make people happier?

Bible encounter

There are many other
relevant passages about
wealth in the Bible.
One way to find these
is to take a look at *The
Poverty and Justice Bible*
published by Bible
Society in 2008 (visit
**shop.biblesociety.
org.uk**).

Within the broader Old Testament tradition wealth was double
edged. It could be viewed as God's blessing for a righteous
life (1 Kings 3.3–15; Job 42.10; Ecclesiasticus 44.6).
Alternatively, it could be a sign of wickedness, especially if it was
obtained illegally or through oppression of others, especially
the poor (I Kings 21; Isaiah 60.8–12; Amos 2.6–8; Proverbs
28.6,8,22). People were expected to use their wealth to
benefit those less well off, such as widows and orphans (see
also Deuteronomy 15.4,7–8 ; 26.12–13).

There are several passages in the Gospels which deal with
wealth: Matthew 6.19–21,24; Mark 10.17–31 (see also
Luke 18.18–30); Luke 19.1–10. Take a quick look at these
passages and notice the different kinds of material we have
here – *teaching* to the crowds or disciples; *instruction* in the
context of (rabbinic) debate; *parables*; *encounters* (perhaps even
a miracle). You might like to allocate one passage each to a
subgroup of two or three people and ask them to relate that
passage to one of the types of material mentioned above; or
ask the whole group to read all four passages quickly and vote
on which is teaching, instruction, and so on.

We can see that Jesus had much to say about wealth,
addressing different audiences and using different styles of
material to communicate his message. It was an important
subject for him.

Key passage: Mark 10.17–31

When studying this passage from Mark, it is helpful to know
about two significant contextual factors concerning poverty
and wealth in the time of Jesus.

Increasing poverty

For Jesus and his contemporaries, wealth was a highly significant
issue, because poverty was in fact on the increase at that time.
Two things were making the plight of the poor more difficult.

• One was the growth of banditry. This was partly the result
  of enforced poverty by Roman taxation, low wages and

lack of work, particularly outside Jerusalem. It seemed to be a case of 'steal or starve'. There was no police force to protect ordinary people, so few people would dare travel alone. The parable of the Good Samaritan is a witness to this problem.

- The other was the process of urbanisation, which – then as now – exacerbated the vulnerability of the poor and emphasised the power of the wealthy. Many ordinary people were in danger of starvation. Added to this, wealth often ensured status, while poverty was seen to indicate rejection by God. So the poor could easily feel and be regarded as completely rejected and worthless.

Contemporary attitudes to wealth

There were also negative attitudes to wealth in evidence around the time of Jesus. The following Jewish texts show this.

- 'If one is excessively rich, he sins.' (Psalms of Solomon 5.16)

- 'Woe to you, you sinners, for your riches make you appear righteous, but your hearts prove that you are sinners … and [you] trample upon the humble through your power.' (1 Enoch 96.4–5)

- 'The princes of Judah are those upon whom rage will be vented … they have defiled themselves … with wicked wealth … and bragged about wealth and gain.' (Damascus Document 8.3–10, one of the Qumran Community documents)

- 'My children, the love of money is a sure path to idolatry … it drives to distraction whoever is in its grip.' (Testament of Judah 19.1–2; this document may have been reworked by Christians)

Jesus' attitude

In a similar way, Jesus appears to have condemned wealth or at least been acutely aware of its dangers – even when the wealth has not been gained 'illegally'. So in our key passage in Mark 10, the man has not even 'defrauded' (see verse 19). This was not technically one of the Ten Commandments – presumably 'defraud' is a functional equivalent to 'covet' – and was typically understood as 'do not withhold the wages of the poor' (see Leviticus 19.13).

Jesus seems to accept that this man had done what

Often the details in the Gospels are fascinating. In his version of the Mark 10 story, Luke omits 'defraud'. Matthew does too, but inserts 'You shall love your neighbour as yourself' (Luke 18.20; Matthew 19.19).

he claimed. His claim might well be more modest than it sounds in English (one translation reads 'I have been careful to observe...'). It is little different from the comment applied to Zechariah and Elizabeth in Luke 1.6, who were 'living blamelessly according to all the commandments and regulations of the Lord'.

The man probably considered that his many possessions were God's reward for him keeping the laws and were thus a sign that, of course, he would have a place in God's Kingdom. If so, Jesus completely reverses this view.

Jesus goes on to indicate that possessions can prevent the possibility of discipleship: *following Jesus* (not law observance or having wealth) is the key to inheriting eternal life (Mark 10.21–23).

Given this appeal to follow him, it is noteworthy that Jesus does not ask the man to give his wealth to the disciples, the community of Jesus' followers, but to the poor.

The disciples' response of incredulity shows how radical Jesus' comment must have appeared to them (Mark 10.23–27). Yet it was also a common Jewish understanding that there would be a reversal of fortune in the 'age to come'.

> Their souls will be made to go down to Sheol, and they will be wretched, and their distress will be great; and in darkness and in chains and in burning flames your spirits will come to great judgment.
>
> (1 Enoch 103.5–8)

Jesus seems to agree with this, at least – see Matthew 6.19–21; Mark 10.21,28–31; Luke 16.19–25.

> **Job 31.16-23** indicates how a generous person should feel responsible towards the poor (various categories of people, including widows and orphans, were considered to be part of 'the poor'), although withholding wages is not mentioned here. The following verses (24–25) present an ideal attitude to wealth.

![icon] Group discussion questions

1. In the light of the Old Testament and passages from later times you have now read, how Jewish does Jesus' attitude to wealth seem to you? Where do you think he might differ from his contemporaries?

2. What seems to have been Jesus' preferred approach to helping people escape from the 'wealth trap'? As well as the Mark passage, you may wish to consider the Zacchaeus encounter (Luke 19.1–10). This follows the disciples' expression of bewilderment: if the wealthy

cannot be saved, who can? Jesus' response is, 'What is impossible for mortals is possible for God' (Luke 18.27). So how significant is this story for us?

3. For the man in Mark 10, is it wealth *per se* or 'slavery' to possessions and the status that wealth provides that is the problem? For instance, it has often been pointed out that it is the *love* of money which is the root of all evil (1 Timothy 6.10). Think this through first in the light of our Gospel passage (what does Jesus intend or imply?), before beginning a more general discussion (what do we think?).

4. In Mark 10.17–31, do the disciples or Jesus best reflect the normal Jewish attitude to wealth and the wealthy?

5. How do you evaluate Jesus' attitude to wealth and the wealthy? (The group can bring in other material from the Gospels or other sources if they think it is relevant to this discussion.)

   a. Does Jesus give out a consistent message, and if so, what is it?   *Give to poor*

   b. How much of what Jesus said (and did) applies to us? What are the implications for us?

 ## Suggestions for reflection

- Think through the challenge of Jesus' teaching for us, (a) individually, (b) as churches, and (c) as members of our nation. Does it require political action in a democracy? Maybe you could write a piece for your church newsletter or something similar.

- How can the Church exemplify the attitude of Jesus to poverty and wealth more clearly? What two things can you do to help this happen?

- Compile a list of people and situations for prayer, such as:

  > your attitude to wealth and possessions;

  > people you know who are trapped by debt or who feel of no value because they are on benefits or unemployed;

  > charities that work to help with poverty/wealth issues, e.g. Christians Against Poverty, Christian Aid, Tearfund, CAFOD.

Jesus and the Law: Divorce

Introduction

In this session we are again considering Jesus' attitudes to Jewish Law. This time we are looking at his position with respect to divorce, as indicated in the Gospels, and in the light of his contemporaries' views. This connects with the internal division within Pharisaism, helping us position Jesus in his proper context. It also enables us to examine in some detail the appropriate Gospel statements. But of course this is an important contemporary issue for us, so we will also engage with some of the issues raised for us today by Jesus' words.

 ## Opening experience

Objective: to help the group develop awareness of the complexity of emotions and opinions which can coexist in our society, as a preparation for engaging with the Gospel materials.

As well as the legal situation relating to divorce, attitudes have changed significantly over the last 20 years in British society. Many of us experience divorce in multiple ways – perhaps as partners, or as children, or as parents, and certainly as wider family members and friends. For some it will be in a professional capacity, as counsellors, solicitors or teachers.

- Share your experiences of divorce as far as you are able and without breaking any confidences.

- Consider together whether and how attitudes towards divorce and divorcees have changed over the last 20 years.

- Discuss whether society or the Bible has influenced these changes most.

Bible encounter

There are various kinds of biblical material which relate to divorce. These include Old Testament passages which form part of the background for the New Testament. Within the New Testament there are sayings attributed to Jesus, stories involving divorcees and then material in Paul, particularly the Corinthian correspondence. We are focusing on the 'sayings of Jesus' in the Gospels.

Some background information will help us interpret these sayings more appropriately.

Jewish texts

Often when the authorities come to Jesus they bring representatives of different positions so that, whatever he says, he is likely to offend one or the other (see e.g. Matthew 22.15–22). What is not obvious from the Gospels is that the Pharisees themselves were divided on many issues, including divorce. The Shammai school (or 'House of Shammai') was generally stricter in interpretation than the Hillel school (or 'House of Hillel').

Their disagreement regarding divorce revolved around Deuteronomy 24.1–4, particularly the line 'but she does not please him because he finds something objectionable about her…'

The House of Shammai said, 'A man should divorce his wife only because he has found grounds for it in unchastity…' The House of Hillel said, 'Even if she spoiled his dish…' Rabbi Aqiba said, 'Even if he found someone prettier than she…' (see Crossley, *The New Testament and Jewish Law*, page 69, quoting Mishnah Tractate Gittim 9.10).

There were therefore two lines of thinking: (a) divorce only for adultery; or (b) divorce if your wife does not please you for any slight reason.

Shammai and Hillel were two eminent and respected Pharisees. They lived around the same time as Jesus. We have information about them only indirectly through later rabbinic literature. 'House of…' is the Jewish way of referring to them and their followers – we might say 'school' (for more information, see Crossley, *The New Testament and Jewish Law*, pages 15–16). Rabbi Aqiba was active in the late first century and early second century. He had very humble origins but is attributed with ordering the Mishnah. He was involved with the Jewish rebellion against Rome in 132–5 AD. Apparently he regarded the leader Bar Kochba as the Messiah.

Jewish practice

Many people are aware that according to the Old Testament, adultery should be punished by death (Leviticus 20.10). There is no evidence that this was the practice, and certainly not in Jesus' time. If a wife committed adultery, it is likely that the husband was required to divorce his wife – the 'practical substitute' for killing her.

Our understanding of adultery today is not quite identical with the Jewish one in Jesus' day. Leon Morris writes about Matthew 5.32:

> Among the Jews a man was not held to have committed adultery by engaging in sexual acts outside marriage unless his partner was herself a married woman.
>
> (Leon Morris, *The Gospel according to Matthew*, IVP, 1992, page 122)

 ## Key passages

The key Gospel sayings relating to divorce are presented overleaf in tabular form in order to help us spot similarities and differences. Quotes here are taken from the NRSV translation.

Ask the group to take a careful look at these verses. It may help to work in pairs. What do the group members note about them? In what ways are they similar, and in what ways are they different? Below are some points to note.

Context

There are at least three different contexts for these sayings.

- The Sermon on the Mount in Matthew – although these verses are missing from Luke's equivalent (Luke 11.17–49).

3 times mentioned

- The 'test' question raised by 'some Pharisees': 'Is it lawful for a man to divorce his wife for any cause?' (Matthew 19.3). This context is closely paralleled by the Mark 10 passage.

- The Luke 16 passage which is in the context of the significance of John the Baptist and the permanency of the Law. Matthew has something like these verses, but the two issues are separated (Matthew 5.17–18; 11.12–13) and Matthew does not include the divorce saying in this context as Luke does.

Once a law has been written y. hard to change a view.

Matthew 5.31-32	'It was also said, "Whoever divorces his wife, let him give her a certificate of divorce." But I say to you that anyone who divorces his wife, except on the grounds of unchastity, causes her to commit adultery; and whoever marries a divorced woman commits adultery.'
Matthew 19.7-9	They said to him, 'Why then did Moses command us to give her a certificate of dismissal and to divorce her?' He said to them, 'It was because you were so hard-hearted that Moses allowed you to divorce your wives, but at the beginning it was not so. And I say to you, whoever divorces his wife, except for unchastity, and marries another commits adultery.'
Mark 10.4-5, 10-12	They said, 'Moses allowed a man to write a certificate of dismissal and to divorce her.' But Jesus said to them, 'Because of your hardness of heart he wrote this commandment for you...' Then in the house the disciples asked him again about this matter. He said to them, 'Whoever divorces his wife and marries another commits adultery against her; and if she divorces her husband and marries another, she commits adultery.'
Luke 16.18	'Anyone who divorces his wife and marries another commits adultery, and whoever marries a woman divorced from her husband commits adultery.'

In itself the variety of contexts is not too surprising. It suggests that divorce issues, then as now, were a common but complex and contested matter.

The unusual: Mark 10.11-12

Normally the situation presumes that the man will be divorcing the woman – who is usually passive in the process, as in the remarriage processes. But at the end of this Mark passage, the woman is presented as also able to initiate divorce or remarriage. This may reflect the Roman position, but according to James Crossley, there is some Jewish evidence for this too (see *The New Testament and Jewish Law*, page 75, and footnotes 5 and 6 on page 121).

The exception: Matthew 5.32 and 19.9

With Matthew's passages there is the 'except for unchastity' clause which is missing from both Mark and Luke.

So did Mark and Luke assume that adultery was always an acceptable ground for divorce and might even require it? Or were they indicating an even stricter position for Jesus than even the narrow Jewish position? How might we decide between these two possibilities?

Remarriage and adultery: Matthew 5.32

One question here is who causes whom to commit adultery. Matthew implies (by the use of passive verbs) that the person who issues the bill of divorce causes the adultery, and if the other person (the divorced wife) remarries, the issuer of the bill of divorce also causes the adultery for the man who (re)marries her. Thus Jesus always makes the man who initiates the divorce responsible for 'the sin'. This presents Jesus as going further than anyone else – as far as known sources show us. It seems to be a way to protect the status and reputation of the woman, as well as highlighting God's purposes for marriage.

'Certificate of dismissal'

It became a requirement that the man divorcing his wife must give her a *written* document as evidence that she was divorced. This was to prevent the husband divorcing his wife by an oral statement and then (maybe after she had remarried) claiming that she was still his wife, thus establishing (wrongly) that she was an adulteress with the 'new' husband.

The main observations

Jesus in the Gospels seems to recognise the reality of marriage at creation, so deeming it part of God's good purpose for humankind. He also seems to acknowledge the Mosaic Law's provisions for divorce under certain circumstances – although there is uncertainty here. In summary, what exactly Jesus intended and its implications for the Christian community are not very clear. (And if we add in 1 Corinthians 7.10–17, the situation becomes even more complex!)

What you might miss

What this presentation of the Bible passages does not show is that in the Greek manuscripts there are also many variations, which probably indicate an attempt to smooth over the apparent differences. This kind of variation – often where

'Unchastity' literally refers to sexual union with a prostitute, but had come to mean 'sexual union before marriage' and also to include sexual impropriety more generally (note that the NIV translates this as 'marital unfaithfulness'), including adultery – that is, sexual union outside marriage.

one passage that was different is assimilated to another Gospel passage in the manuscripts so there seems to be greater agreement – is not very common elsewhere in the New Testament, so its presence around the issue of divorce probably indicates that this topic was a hot one for the early Church as well as for us today.

 Group discussion questions

1. How Jewish do you think Jesus' attitude to divorce was?

2. How important is it to recognise the differences in the Gospel words about divorce? What do you make of these?

3. Jesus' sayings seem to indicate that he took quite a hard line over the acceptability of divorce, probably to protect women from the exploitation that the Hillel school 'encouraged'. What might be the implications for us?

4. How can churches and individual Christians both uphold the sanctity of marriage and be compassionate and helpful to those whose marriages are breaking down or who are divorced?

5. Should churches agree to remarry people when one or other of them is divorced? What does our decision on this question imply to those seeking marriage, (a) about God's grace, and (b) about the Church's mission?

 Suggestions for reflection

• Make a list of people you know who are involved in divorce situations – husbands, wives, children, grandparents – and pray for God's grace and protection for them.

• Find out about organisations which seek to help people cope better with separation and divorce, e.g. Relate, contact centres, solicitors (see below for some suggested websites to visit).

Useful resources

Relate, 'the relationship people', www.relate.org.uk

NACCC, National Association of Child Contact Centres, www.naccc.org.uk/

Family Mediation Services, http://www.direct.gov.uk/en/Governmentcitizensandrights/
Divorceseparationandrelationshipbreakdown/Endingamarriageorcivilpartnership/Planningadivorce/DG_

Making Sense of Jesus: Popular Views

Introduction

The last two sessions have shown us that Jesus often engaged the Pharisees and teachers of the Law on their own terms. He himself was treated as a teacher or rabbi, and this was understandable: he explained the Law, he argued with other teachers and he had a group of disciples, as rabbis did. However, it is clear that Jesus was perceived to be more than an ordinary rabbi. He had a different kind of authority. So the vital question – then, as now – is 'Who is he?' Opponents, the crowds and his own disciples all asked this question. In the next two sessions we shall join them in seeking an answer – within the Jewish 'categories' that would have been familiar to people of Jesus' day. We shall look for these mainly in the first three Gospels, as these offer us the most straightforward access to the 'Jewish Jesus'.

 ## Opening experience

Objective: to sensitise people to the way categories and titles can both convey meaning and, at the same time, confuse understanding!

We all have a tendency to try to make sense of unusual characters or people we see as 'different' by relating them to categories of people we already think we know.

- Invite group members to suggest contemporary 'types' – good and bad – that help shape the way we might perceive an individual if they were so described, e.g. bankers, Taliban, travellers, celebs, scientists, charity workers, hoodies, MPs, journalists...

- Try to decide on the key features for these types, from the group members' perspective. This might have more impact if people write down their thoughts first and then share what they have written.

- Discuss how helpful such categorisations are for gaining a snapshot of someone or to communicate to others what that person is like. What are the dangers?

Bible encounter

It is likely that there were many views about who Jesus was. A whole soup of 'characters' or 'categories' appear to have become associated with him. People struggled to pin him down. He did not seem to fit neatly into their boxes. Yet the very fact that they tried hard to make sense of him indicates his importance. Some viewed him as a threat, and others experienced his help. Different perspectives like these affect how we see someone.

Key passage: Mark 8.27–33

These few verses provide insights into some of the attempts people made to answer the question of who Jesus might be. The titles and functions attributed to Jesus by various people, as relayed by the disciples, are all known to be Jewish. They also show, however, that people were drawing on many different Jewish traditions to come up with plausible answers.

John the Baptist

First they related Jesus to a recent 'celebrity', John the Baptist, around whom a mystique quickly developed. John was a great draw, and he was associated with Elijah, particularly in his role of calling people back to God. In some ways this is surprising because there is no suggestion that John announced droughts, performed miracles, destroyed the opponents of God or acted as a king-maker as Elijah had done. But the association was probably made for two reasons. One was that John appeared, apparently out of the blue, as a rather wild and enigmatic

For more information about John the Baptist (and Elijah), see Matthew 3.1–12; John 1.19–25; also see Matthew 9.14–17; 11.2–19; 14.2; Luke 1.11–17; and Malachi 3.1–4; 4.1–6.

Elijah's ongoing influence can be seen in Ecclesiasticus 48.1-11. Ecclesiasticus is a book you can find in the deutero-canonical books, or the Apocrypha. In this book, Elijah has almost as many verses as Solomon (47.12-25), while Isaiah has seven (Isa 48.19-25) and Jeremiah three (Jer 49.5-7).

Notice that Jeremiah is strangely absent from 2 Kings, whichcovers the time of his prophecies (see Daniel 9.2; 2 Maccabees 15.14-15; the so-called Letter of Jeremiah; and 2 Esdras 2.18).

It is rather surprising that Jesus is not clearly identified with Moses. Moses was also considered a prophet (Deuteronomy 18.18). Supremely Moses was the deliverer of Israel from Egypt and the law-giver, and Matthew seems to present Jesus as the new law-giver. This connection might be implicit in the transfiguration accounts (Luke 9.30-33) and possibly elsewhere. He is certainly not linked with the priests. 'Jesus remained utterly anchored within first century Judaism. His place there ... was the place of a prophet' (NT Wright, The Challenge of Jesus, SPCK, 2000, page 51).

personality, spending time 'in the wilderness'. The other was that a tradition grew up that Elijah would return to earth in preparation for the Messiah who would deliver Israel from occupation.

Jesus is seen as somehow very similar to John the Baptist – even by Herod. As with John, there may have been speculation that Jesus could himself be the Messiah, but this was not stated in so many words.

Elijah and Jeremiah

These two distant historical prophetic figures were familiar to the people through their Scriptures – Elijah from 1 Kings 17—2 Kings 2, and Jeremiah from 2 Chronicles 35.25–36.22 and the book of Jeremiah.

Elijah was thought of as having not died (see 2 Kings 2.11–12), so expecting his return to earth was not problematic. But Elijah also had an 'afterlife' within the Old Testament (Malachi 4.5–6) and in later writings too. That is, we can see that his story was treasured and then developed in people's memories, and so continued to influence their hopes and behaviour. Eventually at the Passover a chair would be left empty for Elijah's return.

Jeremiah we know of mainly through the prophetic book which bears his name, but he also appears in the accounts of 2 Chronicles. Jeremiah came from a priestly family but was called to be a prophet as a young man. He worked at the time when Jerusalem and Judea were threatened and overrun by the Babylonians. They took many of the leaders off to exile in Babylon. Jeremiah told the exiles to settle down there, but also promised deliverance. He too had an afterlife and developed a role in preparation for the Messiah similar to Elijah's.

The prophets

Then comes a rather more general category of 'the prophets'. Probably people were thinking of the Old Testament prophets, but Jewish military deliverers, like John Hyracanus, were also attributed with prophetic gifts.

Jesus does not accept the identification with specific prophets like Elijah or Jeremiah, but he does seem to locate himself among the prophets. This is not a title which gained popularity in the early Church, however, and it rapidly decreased in use.

Although not mentioned in our key passage, there are two other different titles to consider.

Miracle-worker and exorcist

Jesus is known by stories and sayings as a miracle-worker and exorcist. His followers, the crowds (Mark 1.32–36), his opponents (Matthew 12.22–24, 38–39) and some influential figures (Matthew 14.1–2; Luke 23.6–9) all seem to acknowledge this. And Jesus himself presents this as a critical part of his mission (Luke 4.16–21; compare 7.18–23).

For many Christians the miracles of Jesus seem essential for establishing his unique status. There were, however, others doing *similar* things around the same time and, of course, there were plenty of biblical examples (of healing, if not of exorcisms). Whether there was anyone doing as many or doing them in the same way is by no means clear.

For more on Jesus and his association with prophets, see Matthew 13.57; 23.37; Mark 6.4; Luke 4.24; 13.33–34; John 4.44. The early Church also seems to have affirmed this – see John 4.19; 9.17; Acts 3.22–26; 7.37.

Rabbi

Jesus is frequently referred to as 'teacher', both in the Greek and sometimes the Aramaic form (Mark 9.5, 38; 11.21; 12.32; 14.45). For Jesus it did not (as with Paul) imply formal training or 'ordination'. Both his disciples (who were the teacher's 'learners') and others call Jesus 'teacher'. There is also a recognition that he had his own unique style – especially in terms of authority. Again he seems to have accepted this descriptor. He only queried it when he was called 'good teacher'!

Interestingly, Josephus sees Jesus as a 'wise man' (*Antiquities*, 18). This is not such an obvious title for us today. In many ways (e.g. his pithy sayings) Jesus speaks as a wise man, and Luke describes Jesus as increasing in wisdom (Luke 2.40, 47, 52). Yet, although this would have been a natural ascription, there is almost no evidence to indicate that this term was applied to Jesus – even though it became significant in certain parts of the growing early Church (1 Corinthians 1.24, 30; compare also Colossians 1.15–20).

Group discussion questions

1. What truth do you see in each of the Jewish titles that his contemporaries attributed to Jesus?

2. Why do you think some occur only or mainly in the Gospels (e.g. prophets, miracle-worker), while others continue into the epistles (Messiah or Christ), and some are developed within the epistles (Lord, Saviour, high priest, the Lamb of God, Alpha and Omega)?

3. What titles of Jesus are prevalent in our hymns and songs? You might like to compare a particular writer (e.g. Charles Wesley) or a period of time (e.g. the 19th century) with contemporary songs. Have the terms changed with time?

4. Think about our ways of defining or naming who Jesus is. How do they connect with the Jewish approach of his contemporaries?

 ## Suggestions for reflection

- Note down your favourite titles for Jesus. Take a few moments to ask yourself, (a) where these titles come from (e.g. songs, the Bible, etc.), (b) why they appeal to you, and (c) what aspects of who Jesus was/is might not be included in them. Now maybe use these in a prayer.

- Select an image of Jesus that appeals to you (or design or paint your own) and write an explanatory piece about this.

Making Sense of Jesus: the Disciples and Jesus

Introduction

Jesus asked the disciples, 'But who do you say that I am?'

The title which Peter gave to Jesus and which Jesus seemed prepared to accept for himself was *Messiah*. This, in its Greek form of *Christos*, became the dominant lens for understanding Jesus in the churches, at least those that are represented by the New Testament writings. This is quite strange, as most of the churches were mainly full of Gentiles and *Christos* would not mean a lot to them, certainly not as much as to the Jews. Just because this became the common description for Jesus, we can easily forget its Jewish origins. For the Jews in the time of Jesus there was a range of understandings of the term 'Messiah' which we will explore.

 ## Opening experience

Objective: to alert people to the facts that (a) it is difficult to categorise ourselves in ways we think adequate, and (b) even when we try, not all will see us, or the categories we use, in the same way.

- Give each person in the group a sheet of paper and ask them to write down up to six words to categorise themselves: e.g. white, British, working-class, fashion conscious, mother, black, Afro-Caribbean, professional, jazz lover, artist, etc.

- Then collect up the sheets and redistribute them to different people. In turn each person then reads out the description they now have. People can guess who it is and then discuss together how accurately they think it represents the actual author. Please ensure that the author has plenty of time to comment for themselves!

- Does this exercise help us understand the dilemma Jesus had in accepting other people's descriptions (especially 'Messiah') for himself?

 Bible encounter  *You are The Christ*

People other than Jesus were also linked to the title 'Messiah'. We know from Acts 5.36–37 and Josephus, the Jewish historian who wrote about Judas from Gamala (*Antiquities*, 18.1.1) and Theudas (probably different from the one mentioned in Acts – see *Antiquities*, 20.5.1), that there were other people who were thought of or acted as and claimed to be the Jewish Messiah. Judging from Jesus' comments (see Matthew 24.23–26), this may have been a much more frequent occurrence than these passages suggest.

BUT

We can see from the passage in Session 4 that the term 'Messiah' is critical for the disciples' understanding of Jesus. Contemporary research has shown us that there were many views in the time of Jesus about the nature and role of the Messiah, or about those who would fulfil 'messianic' functions. NT Wright summarises this well:

> Modern scholarship has made one thing quite clear: there was no single monolithic and uniform 'messianic expectation' among first century Jews … we cannot say what, if anything, the average Jew-in-the-market-place believed about a coming Messiah.
>
> (NT Wright, *The New Testament and the People of God*, SPCK, 1992, pages 307–8)

One commonality with all aspects of the 'Messiah' was that in some way or other he was seen to be involved in bringing in the new age, 'the age to come'.

Technically, 'Messiah' meant 'anointed one'. Often the Messiah is linked to Old Testament passages about the coming Davidic king. This role might include restoring God's people to their proper position, in relationship to God and the nations, the restoration of the temple and the defeat of Israel's military enemies. Some prophets and priests were also anointed to their positions. So 'Messiah' or 'anointed one' could cover kings, priests and some prophets. In Qumran (where the Dead Sea Scrolls have their location) some of the community expected both a priestly and a military/regal Messiah.

So, although any one person might think they knew what

they expected from the 'Messiah', there were enough variants around for the term to be malleable. Hence Jesus goes to work straight away to reshape what may well have been in Peter's mind when he said 'Messiah'. — *hence v. 33.*

 ## Key passage: Matthew 16.15-22 *Ch 16 14-17*

In this passage Jesus begins with a strong affirmation of Peter's insight that the disciples think Jesus is the Messiah. By contrast, in the equivalent verses in Mark (Session 4's key passage) Jesus seems very abrupt in his response to Peter (Mark 8.29–30).

To help the group get a feel for what the Messiah was likely to mean to people, look up Mark 13.20–21; Luke 24.19–21; and John 1.40–41,48–49. How do these passages relate to the background information above?

In contrast to the popular views, and even Peter's, Jesus knew that his messiahship would involve suffering, and he seems to have been powerfully influenced by passages from Isaiah, such as Isaiah 53. Later on he uses the Scriptures to show people where the true understanding of 'Messiah' was to be found (see Luke 24.26–27; also Acts 17.2–3,11; 18.28).

It is clear that the disciples – and more generally their contemporaries – really struggled with this essential link between the Messiah and suffering. This was probably because they focused on the role of the Messiah in delivering Israel from her oppressors. Sometimes they used very vivid and colourful language to describe this. Here is an example.

> Behold, O Lord, and raise up unto them their king, the son of David...
> And gird him with strength that he may shatter unrighteous rulers,
> And that he may purge Jerusalem from nations that trample her down to destruction...
> He shall destroy the godless nations with the word of his mouth...
> And he shall have the heathen nations to serve him under his yoke...
> (Psalms of Solomon, first century BC)

Imagine how this would make you feel towards Romans parading their power in Jerusalem!

Perhaps in view of these difficulties of interpretation, Jesus seems to have preferred another title to describe himself.

Son of Man

In Matthew 16.13 we find Jesus referring to himself as the 'Son of Man', where Mark has 'I' at Mark 8.27. In Mark 8.31 there is 'Son of Man', where the equivalent in Matthew 16.21 is 'he'.

It seems likely that Jesus preferred the ascription 'Son of Man' when he was identifying himself. (Interestingly, although we tend to capitalise the title, in neither Aramaic nor Greek were upper case letters used to indicate a specific individual or a recognised title.) Why this is so and what this title meant to Jesus are hotly debated topics. In Aramaic it might be simply an idiomatic way of saying something like 'as for me, myself' (emphatic self-reference), or even 'human beings' (generic), or a combination of both ('a person in a position such as mine'), but it might have more substantial connotations in view of its use in Ezekiel and especially Daniel and later Jewish literature.

It is possible that Jesus used this phrase for a number of reasons. Sometimes he may simply have used the Aramaic idiom to mean himself, but he may have used the phrase on other occasions because it enabled *him* to fill out the meaning even more than was the case for 'Messiah'. So rather than the term defining him, his behaviour, teaching and persona defined the term. *also*

Another advantage of this term was that it did not leave him open to the charge of blasphemy (as 'Messiah' and maybe 'Son of God' would have done), but at the same time he could be hinting at, or leaving open the possibility of, a supernatural role.

As with 'prophet', and in contrast to 'Messiah' (or the Greek form 'Christ'), 'Son of Man' does not feature prominently outside the Gospels (see Acts 7.56; compare Revelation 1.13; 14.14). Once the death of Jesus became an established fact and a feature of Christian faith, the correctives which were clearer in 'Son of Man' compared to 'Messiah' were no longer in doubt. He had suffered and died, so to call him 'Messiah' was the dangerous and provocative thing to do.

It was also, of course, *necessary* to claim that Jesus was the Messiah, otherwise it left open the possibility that there might be someone else who was God's 'first choice' in his redeeming work. Jesus, and no one else, was God's Messiah, but he did not fulfil everyone's expectations of what the Messiah should do and be like!

The term 'Messiah' was often understood as a military punitive conqueror, whereas this was less the case with the term 'Son of Man'.

Group discussion questions

1. How Jewish was Jesus' view of himself?

2. What other New Testament descriptions or titles of Jesus do you recall? Which of these do you value and why?

3. What contemporary categories might help us understand and communicate the reality of Jesus for us today? Here are some ideas to consider: superstar, hero, celebrity, CEO, champion, guru, transformer... What might the dangers be in titles like these? This website may help with your discussion: http://www.rejesus. co.uk/site/module/faces_of_jesus/

4. How tolerant should we be of other people's – even other religions' – ways of perceiving Jesus?

5. When it comes to images and titles of Jesus, how do we distinguish valid from invalid? What criteria can we use?

 Suggestions for reflection

Jesus seems to have been avoiding the militaristic and violent aspects of some people's understanding of the Messiah. Today we are often presented with the 'myth of redemptive violence' – the view that people or even the world can only be rescued by power and violence. See Bible Society's *TransMission*, Spring 1999, pages 7–9, 'The Myth of Redemptive Violence' by Walter Wink, available from Bible Society (biblesociety.org.uk).

- Watch TV or recall films which portray this understanding of salvation through violence, or evaluate government policies and assess how prevalent this is. See if you can spot any stories or approaches which run counter to this view of life.

- Think through ways in which Jesus as a model may help us avoid falling for this myth, both personally and nationally.

- Pray for Christians who are most likely to be tempted by this myth – e.g. those who are being bullied or persecuted, or oppressed minorities.

Jesus and Prayer: the Lord's Prayer

Introduction

> 'We can use a passage as small as the Lord's Prayer to reconstruct some key teaching of the historical Jesus, not to mention the social, economic, religious and political contexts of his time.' (James Crossley, *Reading the New Testament: Contemporary Approaches*, Routledge, 2010, page 65)

In this final session we are looking at one of the most familiar, famous and most used passages from the New Testament – the passage we normally call 'the Lord's Prayer'. There are other prayers of Jesus recorded in or hinted at within the Gospels. Yet, although this is the longest we have by far, the context in Luke indicates that it was primarily for use by the disciples, so in that sense it might be more accurate to describe it as 'the Disciples' Prayer'. It also came to be used to instruct new disciples during their period of preparation for baptism – and it contains the key teaching of Jesus.

 ## Opening experience

Objective: to remind people of the different forms of the Lord's Prayer and to generate some awareness of the way 'liturgical' use might impact the biblical text.

- Ask each group member to write out at least two versions of the Lord's Prayer with which they are familiar, and place them on the floor or table so that everyone can see them.

- Ask the group to share their thoughts about the differences between versions. What variations can they spot? If possible, note these differences on a large piece of paper or flip chart. Among these, the most noticeable might be the use of 'thee'/'you', etc. Of more consequence are the following: (1) 'hallowed'/'holy'; (2) 'trespasses'/'sins'/'debts'; (3) 'temptations'/'trials'/'testing'; (4) the omission or inclusion of the liturgical ending, 'For yours is the Kingdom, the power and the glory, for ever and ever, Amen'.

- Invite people to suggest/explain why these differences occur.

Bible encounter

The Gospels have quite a lot to say about Jesus and prayer. All the Gospels, but especially Luke, indicate that Jesus prayed a lot (Luke 3.21; 5.16; 6.12; 9.16,18, 28–29; 10.21–22; 11.1; 22.32,40–41; also Luke 22.17–19; 23.34, 46) and also that he had much to say about prayer, often in his parables.

It is likely that Jesus followed the Jewish practice of having three prayer times a day (see Daniel 6.11). It had become the custom that all Jews would pray the '18 Benedictions' and recite the Shema (see Deuteronomy 6.4–9) in the morning and evening, and at 3 pm only the '18 Benedictions'. They would also add their own petitions. We can see from Acts 3.1 that the earliest Church followed this approach.

'We know that he [Jesus] participated in the liturgical heritage of his people ... The three hours of prayer in particular were so universally observed among the Jews of Jesus' time ... So we may conclude with all probability that no day in the life of Jesus passed without the three times of prayer.' (J Jeremias, *The Prayers of Jesus*, SCM, 1967, pages 73,75)

Key passages: Matthew 6.9–13; Luke 11.2–4

Our two passages are set out in parallel with the main additions and differences in bold. These are both taken from the Contemporary English Version (CEV).

Matthew 6.9–13	Luke 11.2–4
'You should pray like this: **Our Father** in heaven, help us to honour your name. Come and set up your kingdom, **so that everyone on earth will obey you, as you are obeyed in heaven.**	So Jesus told them, 'Pray in this way: Father, help us to honour your name. Come and set up your kingdom.

Matthew 6.9-13	Luke 11.2-4
Give us **our food for today.**	Give us **each day** the **food we need.**
Forgive us **for doing wrong,** as we forgive others.	Forgive **our sins,** as we forgive everyone who has done wrong to us.
Keep us from being tempted **and protect us from evil.'**	**And** keep us from being tempted.'

Straight away we can see that there are differences in the two Gospel versions. What are the most noteworthy differences? Discuss these amongst the group. Why do you think there are such variations? How much do they matter? It may help you to think about the reasons for differences in contemporary translations, and then test out whether something similar could apply to the differences between the versions in Matthew and Luke.

The disciples' prayer

There is some evidence that the Pharisees and the Essenes developed distinctive prayers for their followers (see J Jeremias, *The Prayers of Jesus*, Studies in Biblical Theology Series 2, No. 6, SCM, 1967, page 77).

Luke indicates that John the Baptist also provided a pattern of prayer for his followers. Unfortunately we do not know what this was, but it does suggest that prayer was one of the distinguishing marks of each rabbi's followers. So this prayer was intended to summarise the distinctives of Jesus' approach to religion and life.

Below is a Jewish Aramaic prayer (the Kaddish). Originally it was used by the rabbis when they had finished giving their sermons (also in Aramaic) on the Sabbath. It is likely that Jesus would have taught this prayer in Aramaic.

Exalted and hallowed be his great name
in the world which he created according to his will.
May he let his kingdom rule
in your lifetime and in your days and in the lifetime
of the whole house of Israel, speedily and soon.
Praised be his great name from eternity to eternity.
And to this, say: Amen.
(Translation from J Jeremias, *New Testament Theology*, 1, Scribner 1971, page 198)

What do you notice as you compare this prayer with the Lord's Prayer?

Our Father

We know that the early Church used *Abba*, the intimate Aramaic word for 'father', to refer to God, and Jesus is reported to have done the same in the Garden of Gethsemane prayer (Mark 14.36; but not in the parallel passages in Matthew 26.38–42; Luke 22.42). Jesus' use of *Abba* is considered to be special. Paul uses it twice in Romans 8.14–17 and Galatians 4.4–6. Both passages are to do with the very heart of Christian identity and the reliance on the Spirit. This suggests that this word is of very particular importance to Christian believers. Paul's comments also imply that using *Abba* was common Christian practice. This is even more remarkable when one considers that most of those addressed would not have been Aramaic speakers.

It seems somewhat surprising, therefore, that Jesus appears not to use *Abba* at the beginning of the Lord's Prayer (or that the Gospel writers did not preserve that Aramaic word when they translated it into Greek). Why this is the case remains a mystery.

> There are a few other Aramaic words that have survived in both Gospels and letters, e.g. *Corban* (Mark 7.11, where a translation is given); *Talitha cum* (Mark 5.41, also supplied with a translation); *Golgotha* (Mark 15.22); *Maranatha* (1 Corinthians 16.22); *Cephas*, Peter's Aramaic name (1 Corinthians 3.22; 15.5; Galatians 1.18); *Boanerges*, the nickname for James and John (Mark 3.17, where a translation is provided).

Debts versus sins/trespasses

It has been suggested that although in English, as in Greek, these words come from distinct realms of discourse ('debts' is a financial term; 'sins' is a religious one), they may both reflect an Aramaic background. In Aramaic the same word can be used of both realities.

Bread for today, the food we need

In both versions quoted above we have the hope for daily bread, although how this is expressed varies. For many of Jesus' contemporaries, this would have been a very earnest prayer as they lived with considerable uncertainty about their next meal.

Perhaps the story of God feeding the Israelites in the wilderness with manna is in the background here too (Exodus 16.1–8, especially verse 4).

However, it soon became normal to interpret the word for 'daily' in a spiritualised sense, linking it to the Eucharist, or to Jesus as the 'Bread of Life'. The discovery of fragments of papyri a hundred years ago then made it clear again that it was a common word for 'every day' (see Eugene Peterson, *Eat This Book*, Hodder & Stoughton, 2006, pages 147–150, for a

> 'Such hope would have been common enough across the ancient world given that the overwhelming majority of rural dwellers would have been close to the breadline. We might add famine and crop failures were unfortunately too common and could have devastating effects (compare Acts 11. 27–30) ... it is possible that land displacement and social and economic changes accompanying the building of Tiberias and the rebuilding of Sepphoris as Jesus was growing up could have contributed to a sharpening of the issues of rich and poor.' (Crossley, *Reading the New Testament*, pages 64–65)

popular account of this story).

It is also worth recalling that 'bread' in Hebrew was used for food generally, and this is reflected in the CEV translation given above.

Temptations, trials, testings

The word translated 'temptations' often appears in more modern versions as 'testings' or 'trials'. This word probably refers to the challenges to keep the faith – commitment to Jesus – which would be tested supremely with his crucifixion. But the bigger context for all of this concerned the struggles which were imagined to be the prelude to God bringing in his 'new age' (see e.g. Mark 13.9–27, especially verse 20).

The thought behind this may also be permissive rather than causative: 'Do not *permit* us to experience testings', rather than 'Do not *cause* us to experience testings'. Even more probably, the emphasis is on God delivering us from these evil times or the evil one. Perhaps the ultimate commentary on these words is the prayer of Jesus in Gethsemane (Mark 14.32–8).

 Group discussion questions

1. How Jewish do you think the Lord's Prayer is – in the light of Jesus' teaching about prayer, the rabbis' practice of providing a prayer to identify their group, and the Aramaic Jewish prayer given above?

2. One scholar calls the Lord's Prayer 'the clearest and ...the richest summary of Jesus' proclamation we possess'. (J. Jeremias, *The Prayers of Jesus*, Studies in Biblical Theology Series 2, No. 6 [SCM, 1967], page 94). Do you think this is true?

3. The following are prominent themes of Jesus' teaching reflected in this prayer.

   a. God as Father

   b. The Kingdom of God being imminent

   c. Not worrying about provisions

   d. The vital importance of forgiveness

   e. The inevitability of testing times

4. Work in pairs (on one topic per pair) to find other Gospel

material about these issues, and any others you have noted. After a few minutes, ask each pair to share their findings with the group. It might be useful to note down the references and hand out copies to everyone. Consider together how Jewish these kinds of topics are.

 ## Suggestions for reflection

- Consider different parts of the world and how people might pray for daily food – in famine zones where they are dependent on handouts arriving, in shanty towns where they eke out a subsistence living, in affluent Britain where so many are obese, among the homeless in our country who are begging for their daily food. How does the lack or abundance of food affect our faith in God?

- How might you pray for people who are undergoing testing times or facing temptations?

Resources for further study

There are many helpful books on the Lord's Prayer, although they often cover the prayers of Jesus and his teaching more widely. Among the best are Sister Margaret Magdalene, *Jesus, Man of Prayer* (Hodder & Stoughton, 1987), pages 161–95; J Jeremias, *The Prayers of Jesus*, Studies in Biblical Theology Series 2, No. 6 (SCM, 1967), pages 83–107.